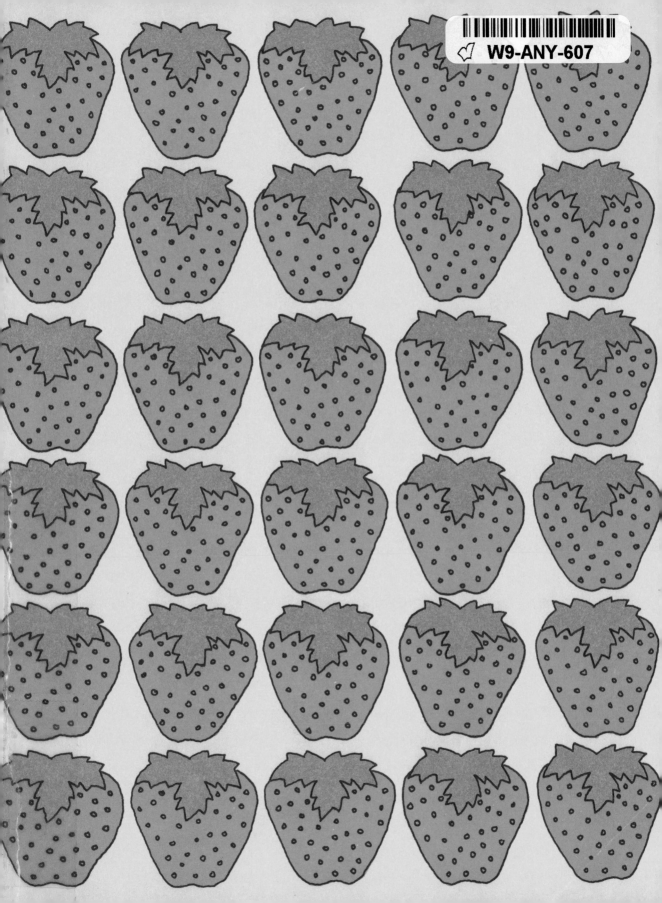

THE STICKYBEAR FAMILY

Bedford Stickybear   **Sara Stickybear**

Bumper Stickybear

**this
strawberry library
of first learning
book
belongs to**

Library of Congress Cataloging in Publication Data

Hefter, Richard.
   Lots of little bears.

   (Stickybear books / Richard Hefter)
   "Weekly Reader Books' edition" – T.p. verso.
   Summary: Little bears teach counting from one to
five and back again.
   1. Counting – Juvenile literature.   [1. Counting]
I. Title   II. Series: Hefter, Richard.   Stickybear
books.
QA113.H427   1983   513'.2 [E]   83-2184
ISBN 0-911787-04-6

lots of little bears

a stickybear™ counting book

by Richard Hefter

Optimum Resource, Inc. • Connecticut

One bear sitting all alone;
Waiting by the telephone.

Two bears sliding on a sled;
One behind and one ahead.

Three bears riding in a car;
They're not going very far.

Four bears playing basketball;
Find the one who is very tall.

Five bears feeling very funny;
Eating jam and bread and honey.

Here are lots of little bears;
Can you count them on their chairs?

Working hard with paint and brush;
Count the bears, they're in a rush.

How many bears can you see;
Climbing around in this big tree?

These bears came to say hello;
Count them please, before they go.

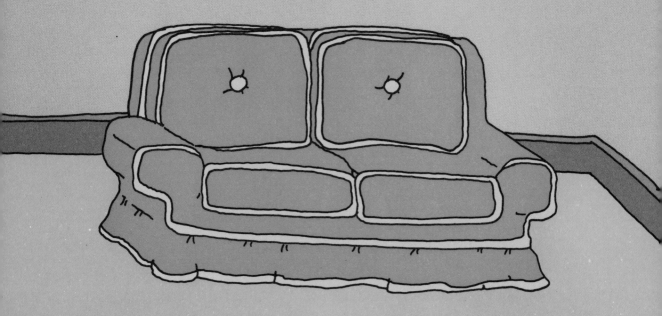

Won't somebody count this bear;
Floating high up in the air?

Bears are going for a drive;
If you count them, you'll find five.

When the rain begins to pour;
Count the wet bears, you'll find four.

How many bears do you see?
They counted each other, there are three.

These bears are trying to hide from you;
If you look very hard, you'll find two.

One bear with a toy to keep;
Tucked in bed, fast asleep.

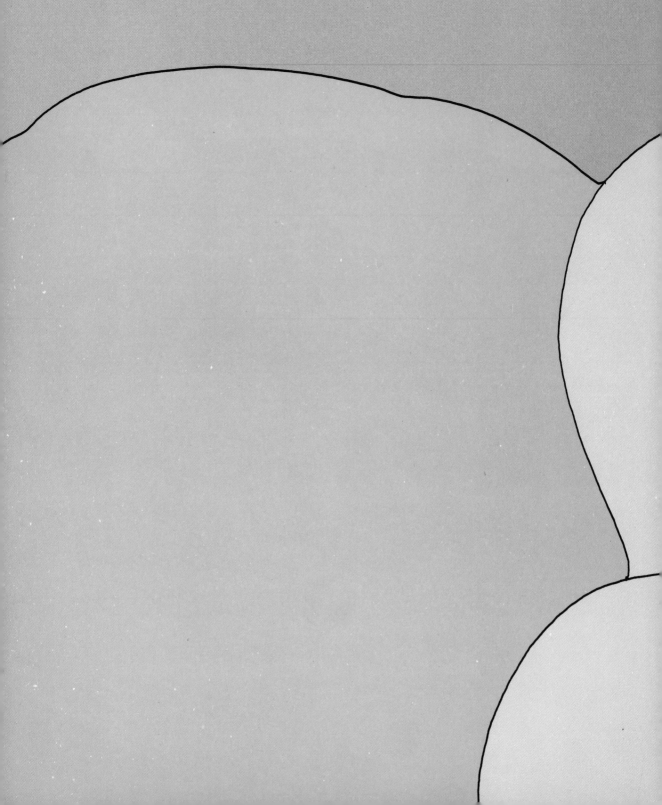

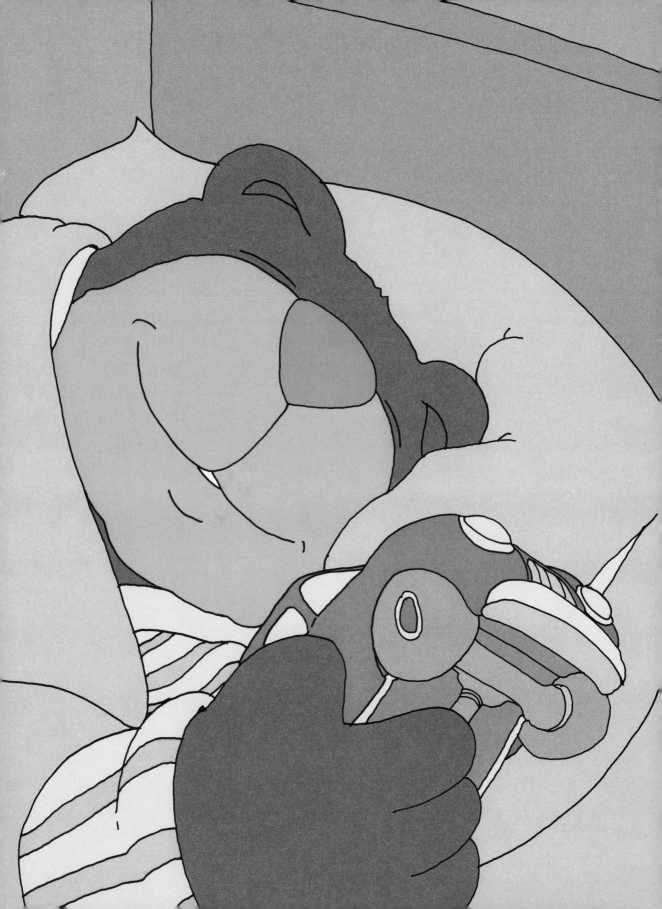

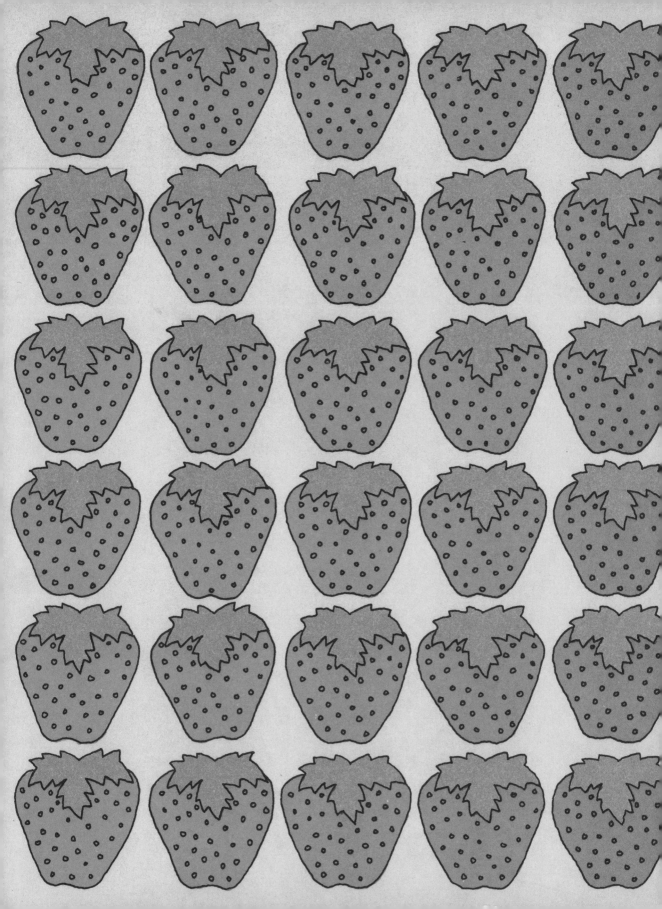